AMBROSIA

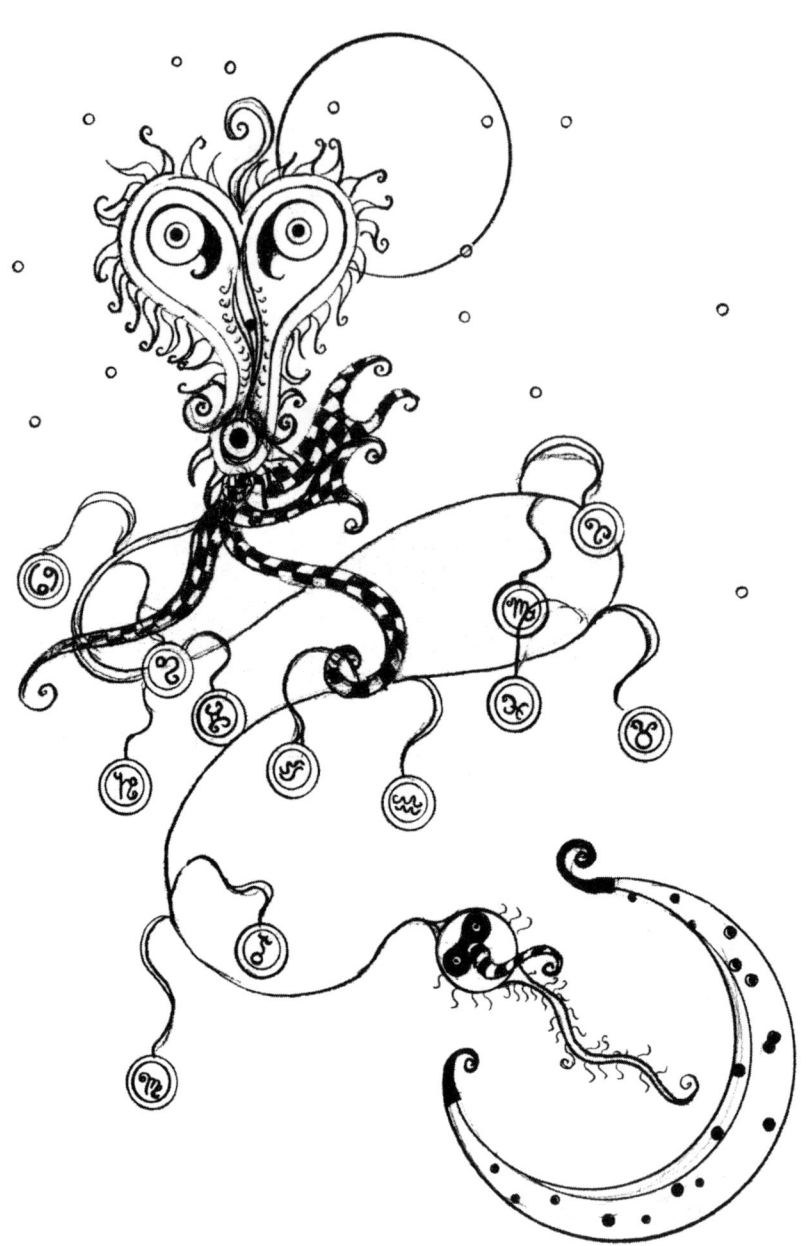

SPIRO

ART OF RAW CUISINE
AMBROSIA

MARC ANTHONY HATSIS

WHITE CROSSLET

Published in 2006 by White Crosslet Publishing Co.

Ambrosia: Art of Raw Cuisine

Copyright © 2006 by Marc-Anthony Hatsis

All artwork copyright © Marc-Anthony Hatsis

No part of this book may be produced or transmitted in any form or by any means, electronic or mechanical, including photocopying, recording, or by any information storage and retrieval system, without written permission from the publisher and/or author.

Printed in the United States of America

White Crosslet Publishing Co and its logo, a crosslet within a square, are trademarks of White Crosslet Publishing Co.

Visit our website at www.whitecrosslet.com

Front cover: Doctor Durian, pencil on paper, 8.5" x 11", 2006

Back Cover: Starfruit- Crosslet, pencil on paper, 8.5" x 11", 2006

Concept and Design by Marc-Anthony Hatsis

Editing: Karen J. Gordon

Typesetting: Clark Kidman

Library of Congress Control Number: 2006925522

Includes Index

ISBN 10: 0-9779797-1-7
ISBN 13: 978-0-9779797-1-4

Disclaimer: The information contained in this book is not intended as medical advice. Marc-Anthony Hatsis does not recommend cooked foods or standard medical practices. The author, publisher and/or distributors will not assume responsibility for any adverse consequences resulting from adopting the lifestyle described herein.

CONTENTS

FOREWORD BY ALEKSEY P. YURENEV, MD, PhD, FACC

NOTE ON ILLUSTRATIONS

INTRODUCTION BY MARC-ANTHONY HATSIS   *1*

◆

AUTUMNAL AMBROSIA   *3*

WINTER AMBROSIA   *31*

SPRING AMBROSIA   *59*

SUMMER AMBROSIA   *89*

◆

INDEX   *111*

LIST OF ILLUSTRATIONS*

Frontispiece   *Dr. Durian with zodiac bevy*

Introduction Page   *Self portrait*

Page 7   *Leo*
Page 9   *Blood Mandala*
page 11   *portobello mandala*
page 13   *Pepper Mandala*
page 17   *Virgo*
Page 19   *Pomagranate Mandala*
Page 21   *Orange*
Page 25   *Libra*
Page 27   *Persimmon Mandala*
Page 29   *Date Mandala*
Page 35   *Scorpio*
Page 37   *Tomato Mandala*
page 39   *Pomagranate Mandala No.2*
page 43   *Sagittarius*
page 45   *cucumber Mandala*
page 47   *avocado mandala*
page 51   *Capricorn*
page 53   *pineapple mandala*
page 55   *tomato mandala no.2*
page 57   *avocado Mandala no.2*
page 63   *aquarius*
page 65   *papaya mandala*
page 67   *banana mandala*
page 69   *banana mandala no.2*
page 73   *pisces*
page 75   *grape mandala*
page 77   *cucumber mandala*
page 79   *starfruit mandala*
page 83   *aries*
page 85   *pomagranate mandala no.3*
page 87   *tomato mandala no.3*
page 93   *taurus*
page 95   *apple mandala*
page 97   *pepper mandala no.2*
page 101   *gemini*
page 103   *fig-cross mandala*
page 107   *cancer*
page 109   *alexandre dumas balancing a spinach leaf on his tongue*

*All of the above illustrations are pencil on paper, 8-1/2 x 11 inches.

FOREWORD

Ambrosia, by Marc-Anthony Hatsis, reminds me of the famous Salerno School of Medicine's *Regimen of Health,* which was one of the most popular poems in the history of both medicine and literature. The work was penned for an anonymous English king and was associated with a work by Aristotle written for Alexander the Great.

Ambrosia provides us with a practical guide for obtaining optimal health through living the raw vegan lifestyle, based on fruit consumption. It is no secret that in the animal world frugivorous creatures live longer than carnivores.

Professor Aleksey P. Yurenev, MD, PhD, FACC

NOTE ON ILLUSTRATIONS

I have used the Mandala form to represent the symmetry of ambrosia (fruit) in the majority of the following illustrations. The frontispiece shows the king of fruits—the durian—donning a flamboyant cravat surrounded by his idolatrous courtiers, acting as a fitting sentinel for the book.

Other images are based on the geometrical beauties inherent in fruit. The rose family, which includes the apple and pear, is based on the number five as can be seen in the pentagonal seed structure of the flowers of all fruit-bearing plants. Five indicates our proper foods and is also the dominant substructure of all living forms. The choicest flowers of love, like the orchid and passionflower, are governed by pentagonal symmetry. The pentagon symbolizes life, particularly human life, and forms the basis of Gothic rose window mandalas.

Marc-Anthony Hatsis

AMBROSIA

INTRODUCTION

"Stop desecrating your sacred body with such an abominable diet. The land around us grows the most exquisite and delicious fruits in plenty. The Earth gives enough nourishment from just its vegetable realm, without the need for torture or violence."

- **Pythagoras**

Raw fruits, along with leafy greens and seeds acting as the basis for your diet cause the least harm to the body, having all of the nutrients that you need to maintain optimal health. No other foods are needed. Ripe fruits are in a predigested state, which can be assimilated quickly, resulting in increased energy and alertness of mind. The body heals itself through a pure diet and by not introducing to it unnecessary things such as supplements and processed foods. Fruit contains in perfect quantity and balance the ideal vitamin, mineral, fat and protein ratios that the human body needs.

Avoiding wrong food choices is essential for well-being. When you embrace raw fruits and vegetables as your exclusive diet, radiant health will appear. A natural diet combined with right thought, speech, and action is the essential way in coming to know yourself. Many people dissipate their energies through unnatural diets, thoughts, and behaviour. There is an alternative course to these ways, which can nourish you instead of leaving you in a perpetual state of craving.

Cooked foods squander the body's precious energies and create imbalances. Dental problems, failing vision, and obesity are the outcomes of indulging in cooked food.

You are what you eat. The less complexity we introduce to our diet and life, the healthier we will become. The simpler the meal, the easier it is to digest.

In addition to diet, there are other elements that are necessary to incorporate for health and balance. These include a clean, harmonious living environment, peace of mind, a loving nature, and sufficient amounts of direct sunlight and clean air.

Most people's sense of taste has been dulled by cooked and highly spiced foods. Our natural senses can be brought back to their original state through natural food choices.

The standard American and European diet is a failed experiment; the existence of indigestion that many suffer from illustrates this fact.

There are no condiments used in the following recipes. Condiments of any kind wreak havoc on the digestive system and camouflage the bland flavours of lifeless, cooked food, making them more palatable.

Many of the following recipes contain only one ingredient. If you make an entire meal out of one type of food, it is called a mono meal. The mono meal is the ideal repast. It nourishes and satiates completely while taxing your digestive system the least. Eating mono meals regularly is the kindest expression that you can offer to your body, allowing you to assimilate your food without potentially disturbing food combinations.

The solution is simplicity. When not eating mono meals, group foods of like kind and eat them sequentially, without mixing, appreciating the essence of each food. Through this method, you can regain the subtle sense of taste that is your birthright. The delicate nuances in raw foods are impossible to come by in cooked food(s). When eating mono meals, your body will give you a direct signal to stop eating. When foods are mixed, the signal of when to stop is never clear; the message your food imparts is confused.

Ideal nutrition can only be gained if your food is consumed in its raw state. Heat destroys nutrients in your food. All enzymes are destroyed at and above 116 degrees. Even steaming requires a temperature above 200 degrees. The cooking process denatures the protein in food. This has been linked to numerous diseases—cancer and heart disease being among them.

We are composite individuals, not a body plus a psyche acting in dissociation. Thus, when we do our best regarding diet, consuming only ripe, raw, and organic foods for our physical well-being, we also are doing the best for our psychic and spiritual well-being.

Marc-Anthony Hatsis

AUTUMNAL AMBROSIA

THREE AUTUMN MENUS

Menu 1 (makes four servings)

PEAR PUDDING

CARROT SOUP

SPINACH SALAD

Leo

PEAR PUDDING

4 d'Anjou pears (peeled and cored)

4 ripe bananas (peeled)

Blend until smooth. Place equal portions in four small bowls.
Serve immediately.

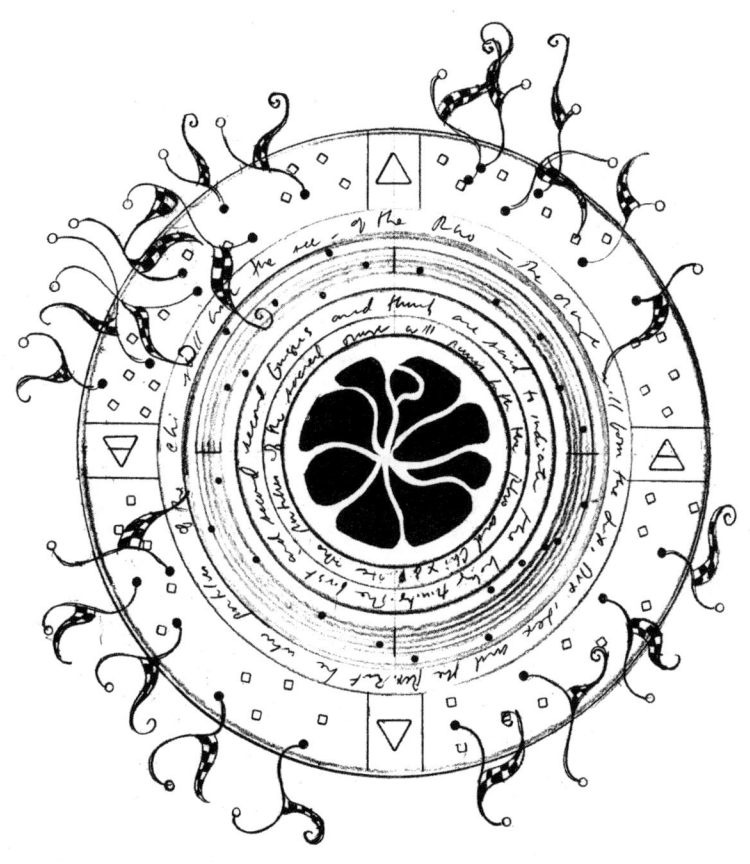

AUTUMNAL AMBROSIA

CARROT SOUP

3 cups fresh carrot juice

1 cup celery juice

4 medium zucchini (peeled and chopped)

4 tablespoons lemon juice

Blend the above ingredients until smooth.
The consistency should be velvety and rich.
Pour liquid soup into four bowls and serve.

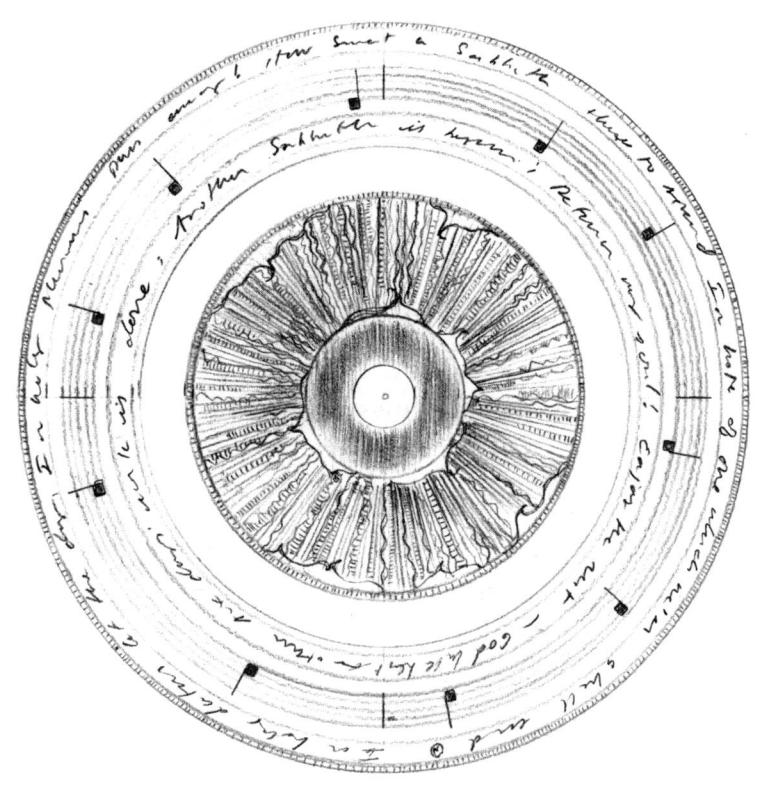

AUTUMNAL AMBROSIA

SPINACH SALAD

2 large bunches cleaned spinach

4 tomatoes

4 ounces raw cashews (soaked overnight)

Blend the tomatoes with cashews.
Divide the spinach into four bowls.
Pour dressing on top and serve.

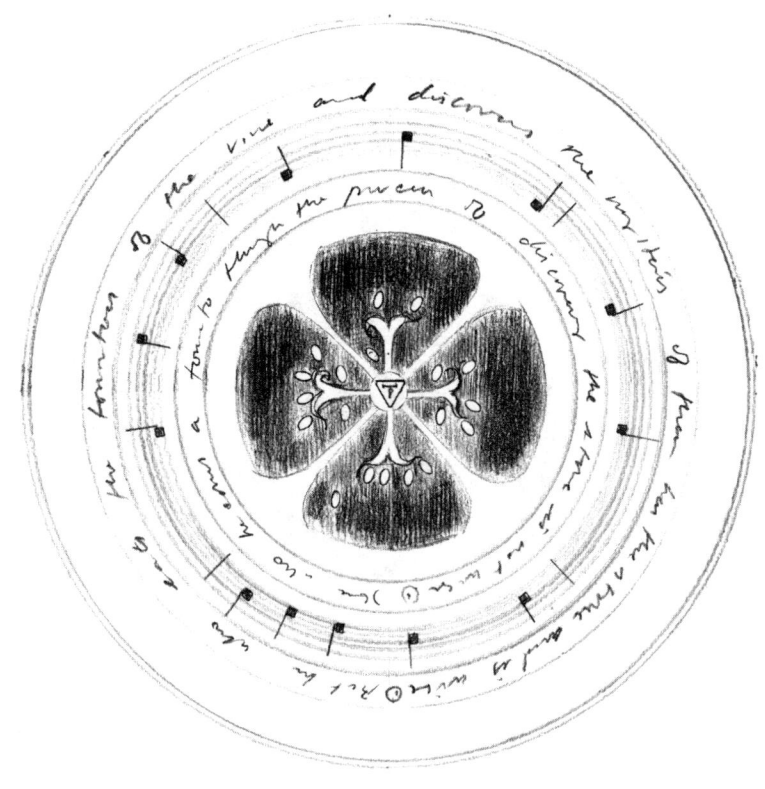

AUTUMNAL AMBROSIA

THREE AUTUMN MENUS

Menu 2 (makes four servings)

BLUEBERRY PUDDING

SALAD ALEXANDRE DUMAS

Virgo

BLUEBERRY PUDDING

4 pints fresh blueberries

3 oranges (seeds and skin removed)

Blend the blueberries and oranges together until smooth
Place pudding in four portions in either bowls or
festive dessert goblets. Serve.

AUTUMNAL AMBROSIA

SALAD "ALEXANDRE DUMAS"

FOR SALAD:

1 cup finely grated and peeled beetroot

1 cup finely grated celery ribs

1 cup finely grated celery root

2 cups finely shredded Boston lettuce

FOR DRESSING:

1 avocado, peeled with pit removed

1 grapefruit, peeled and seeded, chopped

1 small cucumber, peeled

2 celery ribs, roughly chopped.

Place 1/4 of each salad ingredient in the following sequential order on a large dinner plate: lettuce, celery root, celery, and red beetroot. Repeat, making three more plates.

Blend in a high-speed blender all of the dressing ingredients until smooth, spoon a bit of dressing on each salad, and serve remaining dressing on the side. Serve immediately.

AUTUMNAL AMBROSIA

THREE AUTUMN MENUS

Menu 3 (makes one serving)

PERSIMMONS

HONEY DATES

Libra

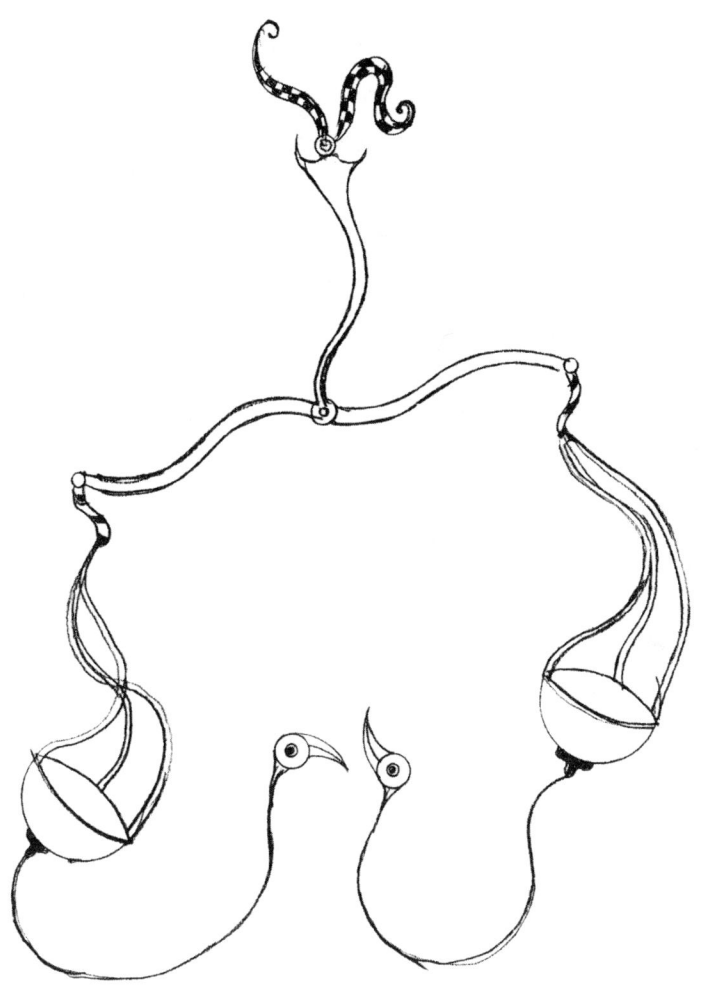

PERSIMMONS

8 very ripe persimmons

Cut each persimmon in half and scoop out
the heavenly fruit with a spoon.

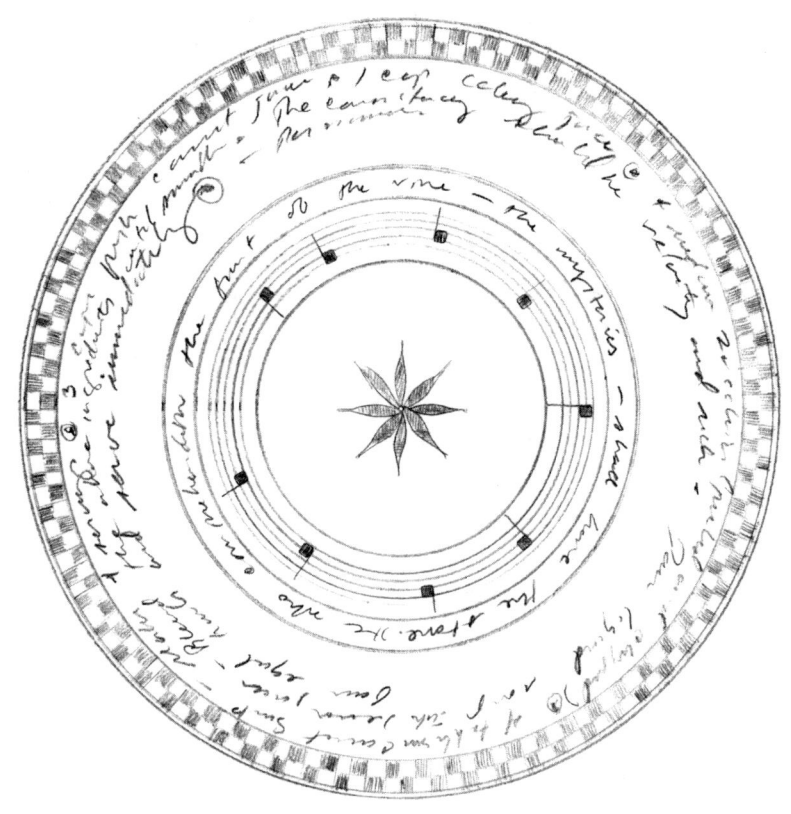

AUTUMNAL AMBROSIA

27

HONEY DATES

5 - 10 honey dates or any other fresh variety

Serve and enjoy.

WINTER AMBROSIA

THREE WINTER MENUS

Menu 1 (makes 4 servings)

BLENDED SALAD

ST. JOHN'S PUDDING

Scorpio

BLENDED SALAD

6 tomatoes

3 ribs celery

4 cups baby spinach leaves

1 handful curly parsley

2 tablespoons lemon juice

Blend ingredients. The texture should be thick and smooth.
Divide equally among four soup bowls and serve.

WINTER AMBROSIA

ST. JOHN'S PUDDING

4 ripe bananas

3 apples

3 tablespoons carob powder

3 honey or Medjool dates

Blend all ingredients and serve in four dessert goblets.
Sprinkle with a touch of carob powder
and serve immediately.

WINTER AMBROSIA

THREE WINTER MENUS

Menu 2 (makes 4 servings)

SATIE SOUP

AVOCADO SAVOURY

Sagittarius

SATIE SOUP

8 ripe bananas

2 medium cucumbers (peeled and seeded)

2 cups chopped spinach leaves

3 honey dates

Blend all ingredients until smooth.
Serve in four soup bowls.

WINTER AMBROSIA

AVOCADO SAVOURY

3 ripe avocados (pitted and peeled)

Juice of one lemon

3 medium tomatoes, chopped

3 cups spinach leaves

Puree above ingredients in blender or food processor
and serve in four small bowls or
dessert goblets.

WINTER AMBROSIA

THREE WINTER MENUS

Menu 3 (makes 4 servings)

PINEAPPLE SOUP

TOMATO SOUP

LEMON PUDDING

Capricorn

PINEAPPLE SOUP

2 pineapples
(skin removed, cored, and cut into chunks)

Blend pineapple until smooth.
Divide among four soup bowls and serve.

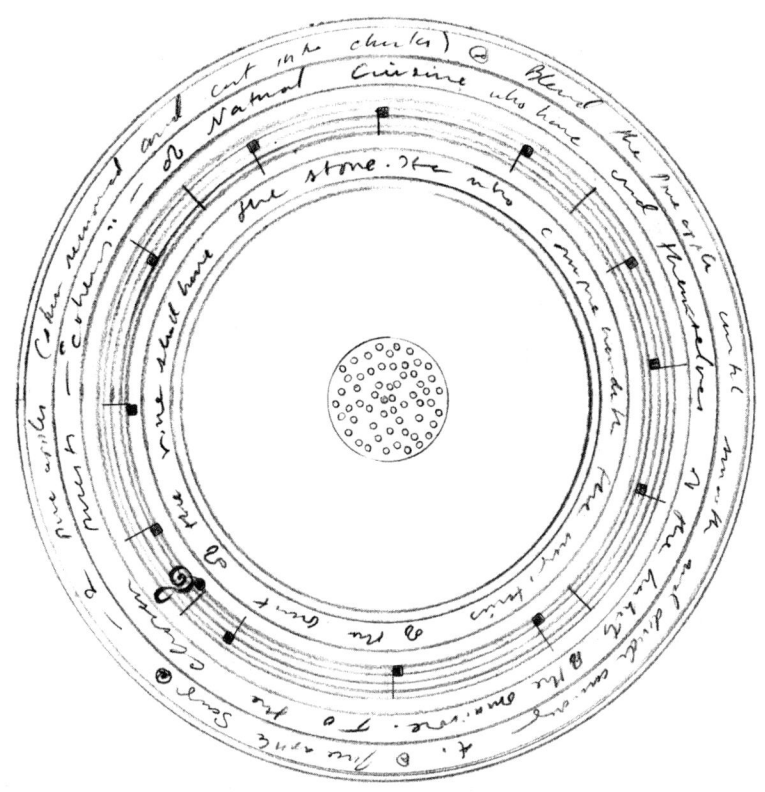

WINTER AMBROSIA

TOMATO SOUP

10 medium heirloom tomatoes

2 Valencia oranges (seeds and skin removed)

3 tablespoons minced cilantro

Blend tomatoes and oranges.
Divide among four soup bowls and serve.
Garnish each serving with cilantro.

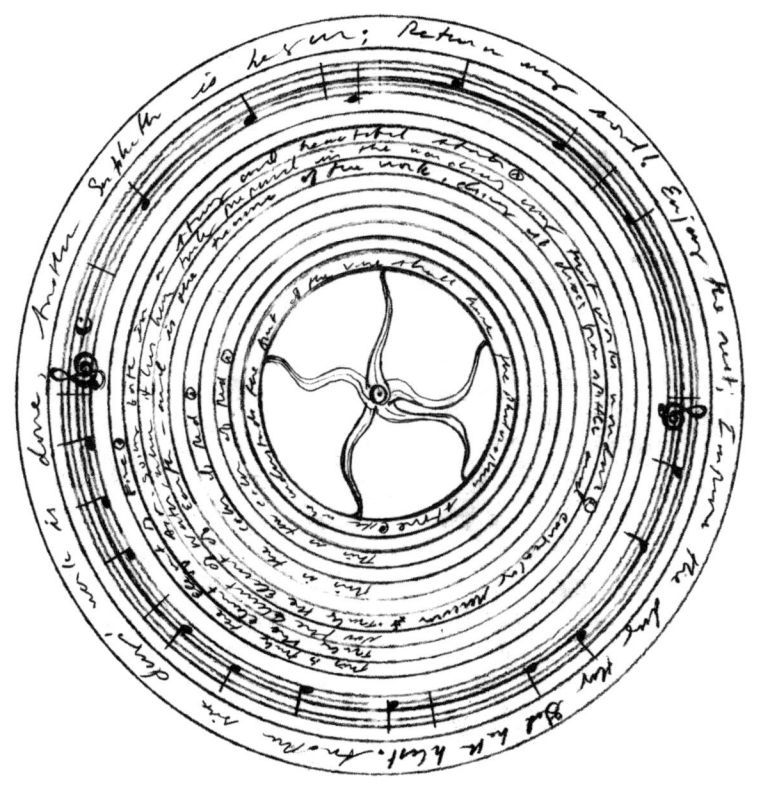

LEMON PUDDING

3 ripe avocados

Juice of one lemon

2 whole oranges (seeds and skin removed)

Blend all ingredients until smooth.
Divide among four parfait glasses and serve.

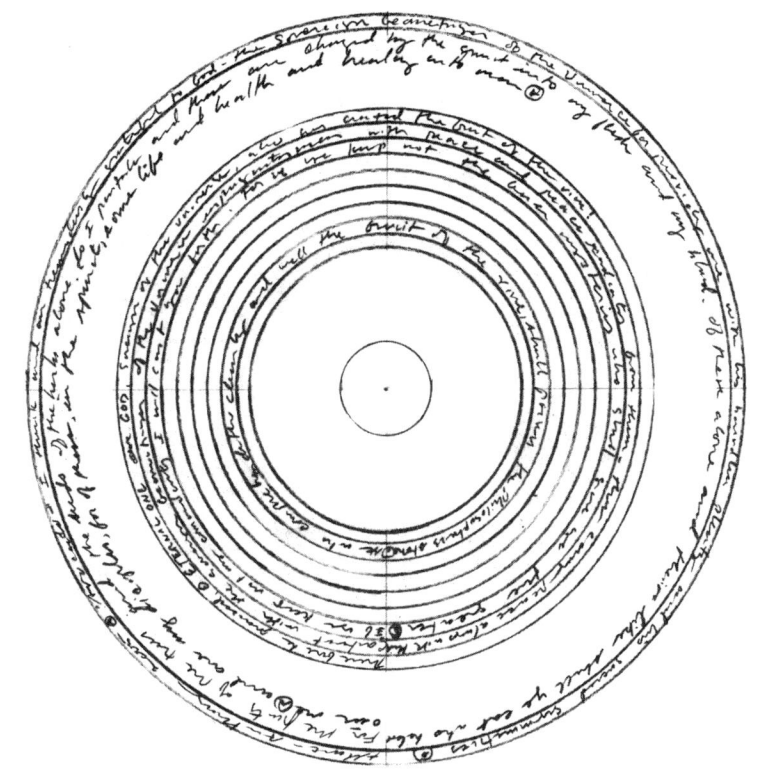

WINTER AMBROSIA

SPRING AMBROSIA

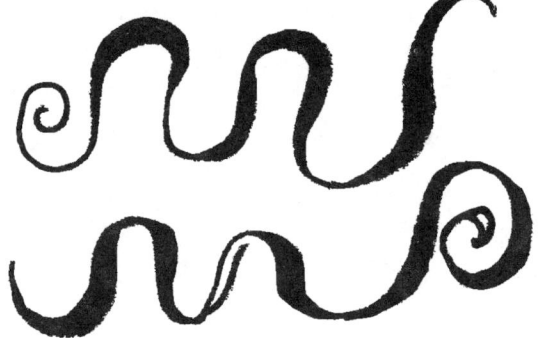

THREE SPRING MENUS

Menu 1 (makes four servings)

PAPAYA PUDDING

BANANAS

MEDJOOL DATES

Aquarius

PAPAYA PUDDING

**2 large papayas
(peeled and seeded)**

Blend papaya flesh in blender and pour mixture into
four large dessert goblets or soup bowls.
Serve immediately.

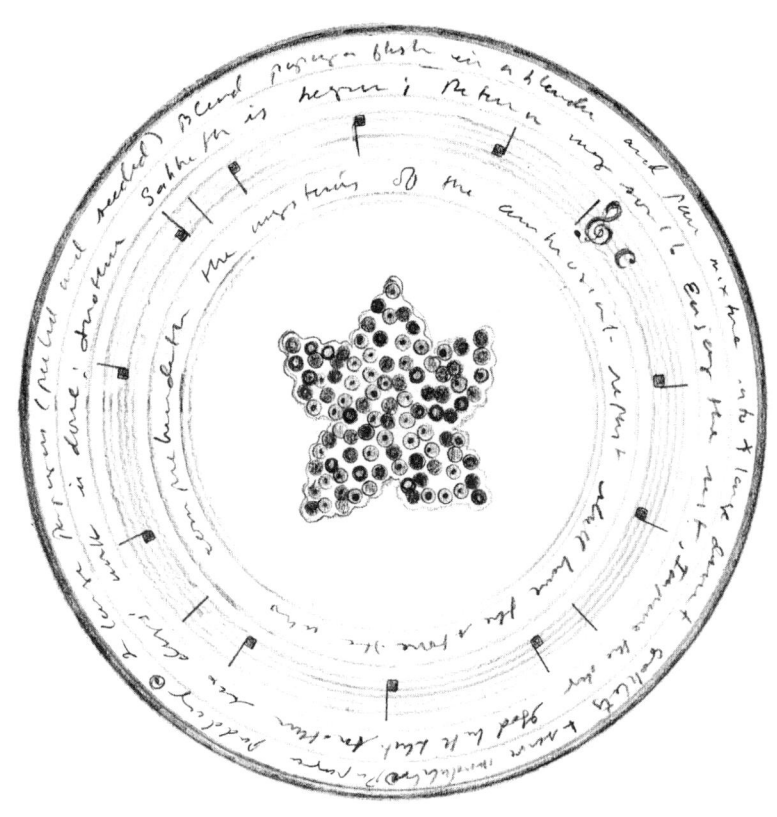

SPRING AMBROSIA

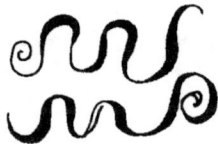

BANANAS

**16 very ripe bananas
(skins removed)**

Divide among four plates and serve.

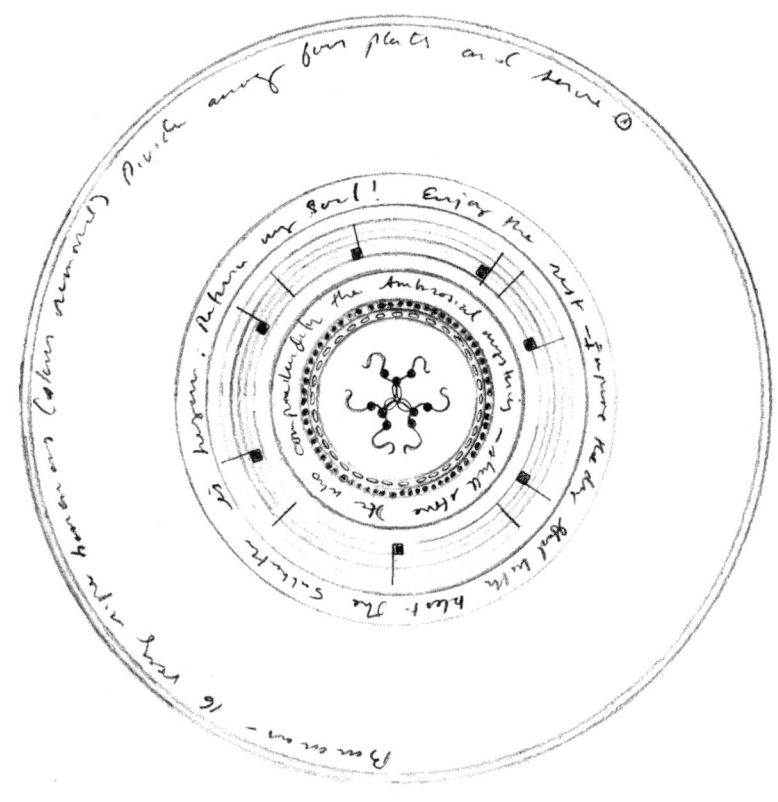

SPRING AMBROSIA

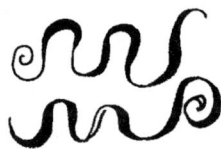

MEDJOOL DATES

20 – 30 Medjool dates

Divide among four small bowls and serve.

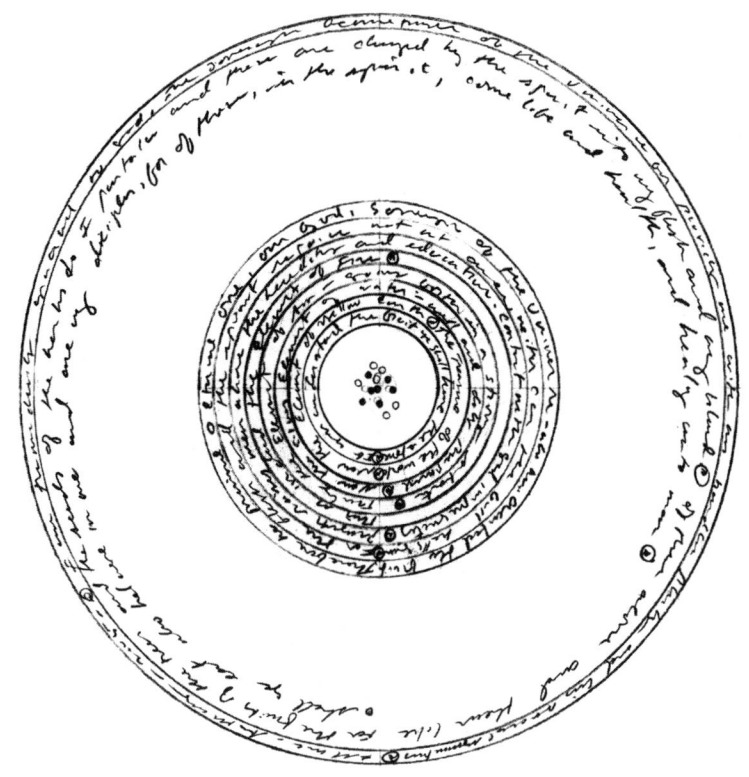

THREE SPRING MENUS

Menu 2 (makes four servings)

GRAPES

CUCUMBER SOUP

AVOCADO, CORN & CUCUMBER SALAD

Pisces

GRAPES

**4 pounds fresh grapes
(seeded/organic)**

Divide among four large bowls or plates and serve.

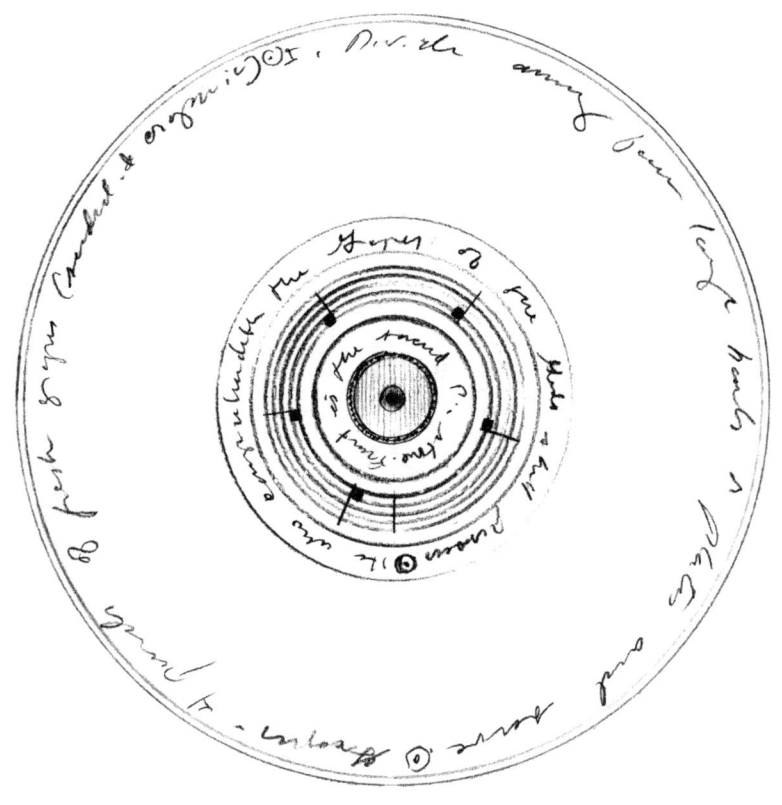

SPRING AMBROSIA

CUCUMBER SOUP

8 medium cucumbers
(peeled and seeded)

Juice of one lemon

Blend above ingredients.
Divide among four soup bowls and serve immediately.

SPRING AMBROSIA

AVOCADO, CORN & CUCUMBER SALAD

Corn & cucumber:

6 ears raw, fresh, young sweet corn kernels
(removed from husk with sharp knife)

1 large cucumber, peeled, seeded,
and minced into 1/8 inch dice

Dressing:

3 ripe avocados (pitted and peeled)

2 tablespoons lemon juice

2 tablespoons water

Mix the corn kernels and cucumber together. Place in mixing bowl.

Blend dressing ingredients in blender until smooth
and pour over the corn and cucumber.
Divide among four plates or soup bowls
and serve immediately.

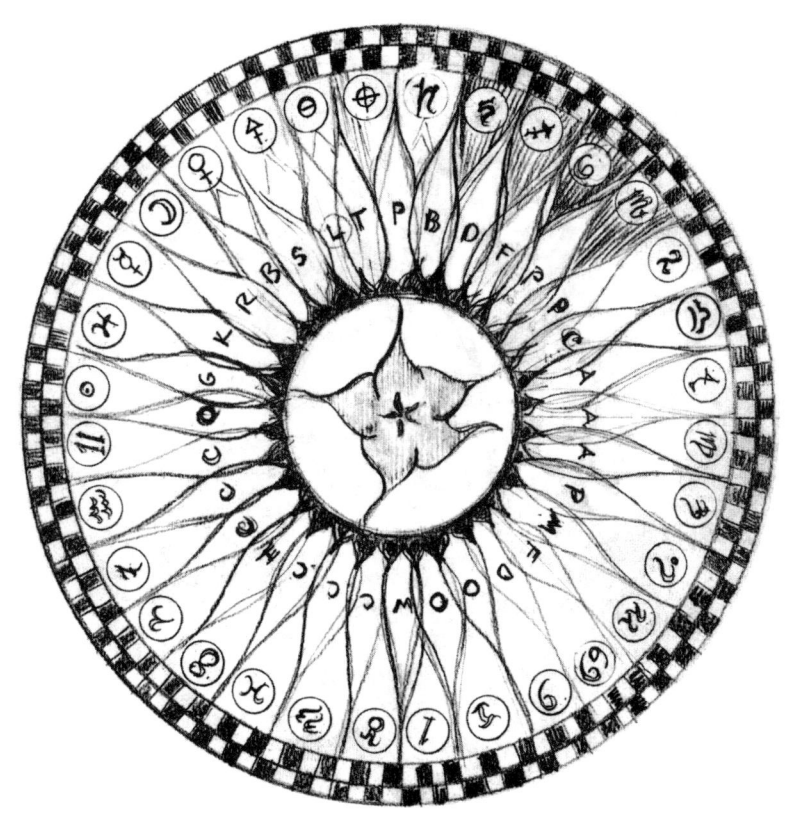

SPRING AMBROSIA

THREE SPRING MENUS

Menu 3 (makes four servings)

MANGO PUDDING

TOMATO SALAD

Aries

MANGO PUDDING

6 ripe mangoes
(peeled, pit removed)

Place mango flesh in blender. Blend until smooth.
Divide among four bowls and serve immediately.

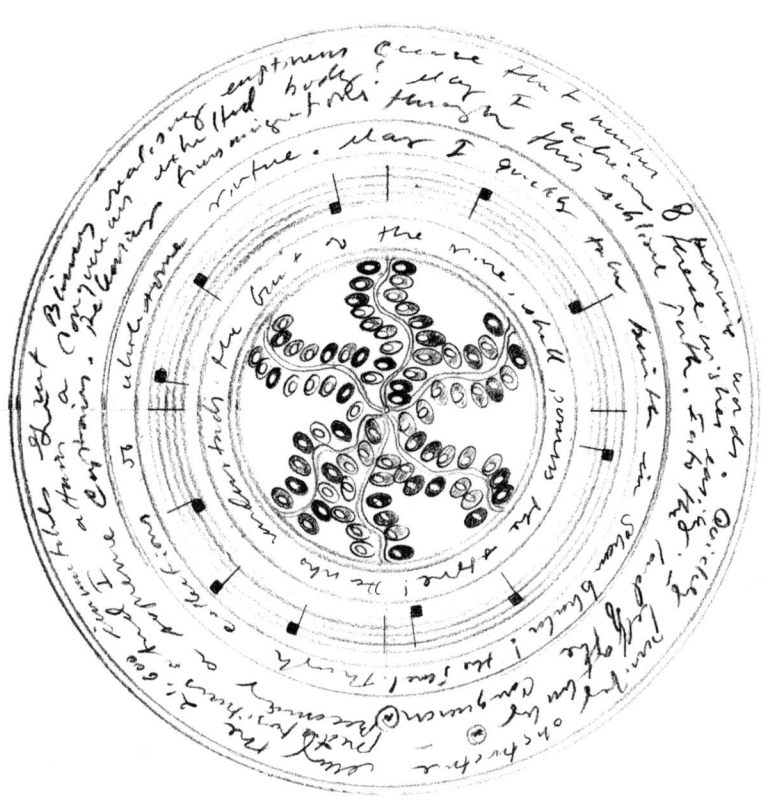

SPRING AMBROSIA

TOMATO SALAD

8 tomatoes (diced)

2 bunches arugula (cleaned and chopped)

1 avocado (diced, with pit and skin removed)

Toss tomatoes and avocado together well.
Serve on top of the arugula on a large platter
and serve immediately.

SPRING AMBROSIA

SUMMER AMBROSIA

THREE SUMMER MENUS

Menu 1 (makes four servings)

CANTALOUPE SOUP

WHITE PEACHES

Taurus

CANTALOUPE SOUP

**4 ripe cantaloupes
(seeded with skin removed)**

Blend cantaloupe flesh in blender.
Divide among four soup bowls and serve.

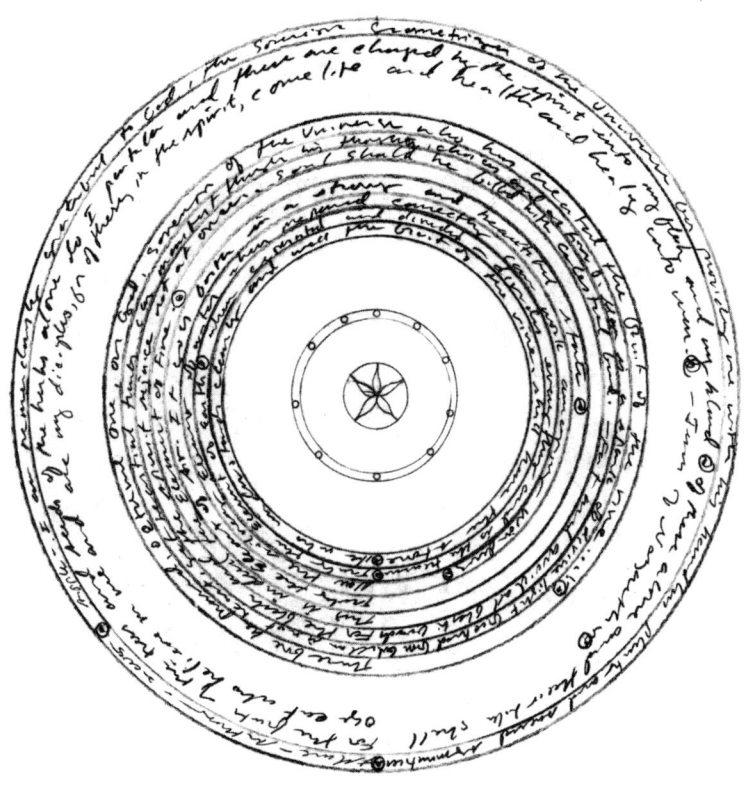

WHITE PEACHES

24 ripe white peaches

Divide among four and enjoy.

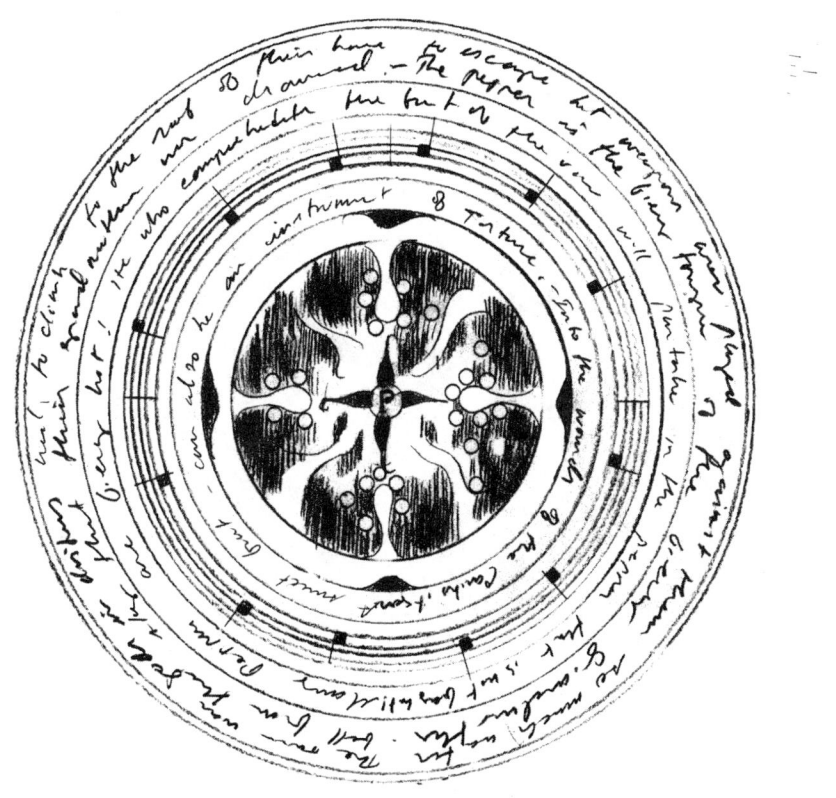

SUMMER AMBROSIA

THREE SUMMER MENUS

Menu 2 (makes four servings)

FIGS

Gemini

SUMMER AMBROSIA

FIGS

40 – 50 fresh ripe figs

Place figs in a large bowl and enjoy
this most perfect mono meal.

Note: with Black Mission figs, I find it preferable to
gently remove the delicate black skin from
each fig before eating.

THREE SUMMER MENUS

Menu 3 (makes one serving)

WATERMELON

Cancer

WATERMELON

1 large watermelon

Slice in half or in smaller sections and enjoy.

PLEASE VISIT OUR WEBSITE AT

WWW.WHITECROSSLET.COM

INDEX

apples
    St. John's Pudding, 38
arugula
    Tomato Salad, 86
Avocado, Corn & Cucumber Salad, 78
Avocado Savoury, 46
avocados
    Avocado, Corn & Cucumber Salad, 78
    Avocado Savoury, 46
    Lemon Pudding, 56
    Salad "Alexandre Dumas," 20
    Tomato Salad, 86

bananas, 66
    Pear Pudding, 8
    Satie Soup, 44
    St. John's Pudding, 38
beetroot
    Salad "Alexandre Dumas," 20
Blended Salad, 36
blueberries
    Blueberry Pudding, 18

cantaloupes
    Cantaloupe Soup, 94
carob powder
    St. John's Pudding, 38
carrots
    Carrot Soup, 10
cashews
    Spinach Salad, 12
celery
    Blended Salad, 36
    Carrot Soup, 10
    Salad "Alexandre Dumas," 20
condiments, 2
cooking, 1, 2
corn
    Avocado, Corn & Cucumber Salad, 78
Cucumber Soup, 76
cucumbers
    Avocado, Corn & Cucumber Salad, 78
    Cucumber Soup, 76
    Salad "Alexandre Dumas," 20
    Satie Soup, 44

dates, 28, 68
    Satie Soup, 44
    St. John's Pudding, 38
diet, 1
disease, 2

figs, 102
fruits, benefits of, 1

grapefruit
    Salad "Alexandre Dumas," 20
grapes, 74

health, 1
honey dates. *see* dates

indigestion, 1

Lemon Pudding, 56
lemons
    Lemon Pudding, 56
lettuce
    Boston, 20
    Salad "Alexandre Dumas," 20

mangoes
    Mango Pudding, 84
medjool dates. *see* dates
mono meals, 2
    Cantaloupe Soup, 94
    dates, 28, 68
    figs, 102
    grapes, 74
    Mango Pudding, 84
    Papaya Pudding, 64
    persimmons, 26
    Pineapple Soup, 52
    watermelon, 108
    white peaches, 96

nutrition, 2
nuts
    cashews, 12

(continued from previous page)
oranges
   Blueberry Pudding, 18
   Lemon Pudding, 56
   Tomato Soup, 54

Papaya Pudding, 64
peaches, 96
pears
   Pear Pudding, 8
persimmons, 26
pineapples
   Pineapple Soup, 52
protein, 2
puddings
   Blueberry Pudding, 18
   Lemon Pudding, 56
   Mango Pudding, 84
   Papaya Pudding, 64
   St. John's Pudding, 38

raw foods, benefits of, 1-2

Salad "Alexandre Dumas," 20
salads
   Avocado, Corn & Cucumber Salad, 78
   Blended Salad, 36
   Salad "Alexandre Dumas," 20
   Spinach Salad, 12
   Tomato Salad, 86
Satie Soup, 44
soups
   Cantaloupe Soup, 94
   Carrot Soup, 10
   Cucumber Soup, 76
   Pineapple Soup, 52
   Satie Soup, 44
   Tomato Soup, 54
spices, 1
spinach
   Avocado Savoury, 46
   Blended Salad, 36
   Satie Soup, 44
   Spinach Salad, 12
   St. John's Pudding, 38

taste, sense of, 1
Tomato Salad, 86
Tomato Soup, 54
tomatoes
   Avocado Savoury, 46
   Blended Salad, 36
   Spinach Salad, 12
   Tomato Salad, 86
   Tomato Soup, 54

vegetables, benefits of, 1

watermelon, 108
white peaches, 96

zucchini
   Carrot Soup, 10